Bucket list
(Noun Informal)

A list of experiences and/or achievements that someone hopes to have or accomplish during their lifetime

Bucket List Journal - things you'd like to do now you're in your 40s.

Published by Verna Scott-Culkin.

Copyright© 2019 Verna Scott-Culkin.

All rights reserved.
No part of this book may be used or reproduced in any manner whatsoever without written permission of the publisher.

ISBN 978-1-9997023-2-8

Find us on Facebook.

Search 'Bucket List Journals Books'.

Also available for 'in your 20s', 'in your 30s' and 'in your 50s'

Contact Us

Instagram - Bucket List Journals
Email - Beforejournals@gmail.com

The charm of starting
a 'Bucket' list
(whatever your age) is
that, just like us,
over time it should
blossom and grow.

People, places, ideas
and experiences.
Don't just think big...

Sometimes it's the
little things that
bring the biggest joy.

These may take a bit of time and patience

Go to a music festival Write a poem or song Test drive a car you've always wanted but have no intention of buying Randomly do a cartwheel in public Sing karaoke Repair something Apologise for something you should have a long time ago Do the splits Random act of kindness Ride in a Hot air balloon Try a new sport Try and learn a new language Develop a party trick Perfect a joke Make your own cookbook Sign on as an extra in a film Stay in bed all day See a wonder of the world Get a tattoo Do a Triathlon Sleep under the stars Ride a motorbike Take part in a protest Go to a dance class Run a marathon Skinny dip Draw a moment from your day every day for a year Visit Bora Bora Take time to smell the roses Pay for someone's meal without knowing them Send a message in a bottle Make a loaf of bread Donate blood Shave your head Speak to someone you don't know (every week) Stay in a see-through igloo Write a book Bury some treasure and a note Volunteer Watch the Sunrise & Sunset in one day Find or create

a signature drink Try and learn a musical instrument Try something you hated as a kid Chase a tornado Grow some veg Perfect a recipe Go horse riding on a beach Swim with sharks Visit the place you were born or your first house Fly 1st class Catch a wave Explore a cave Take a gap year Play paintball Send a thank you card to a boss you liked Ride a zip line Stay on a ranch and herd cattle on horseback Walk over hot coals Go on a yacht in Ibiza Go to a drive-in movie Be on a game show Go to bongo's bingo Take silly photos at Madame Tussauds Surprise someone you love Watch the Northern Lights Find someone with your name Swim with Whalesharks Snorkel over a coral reef Get an invite to a Royal event Ride a mechanical rodeo bull Create a family crest Climb a tree Milk a cow Shear a sheep Start a fire without matches Watch baby turtles hatch on a beach Find a friend from junior school Watch an entire box set in one go Go to a black-tie ball Attend something as a VIP Be successful in your

business Jump in pool fully clothed
Sell a piece of art Get thrown out
of somewhere Dance on a bar Go to
an art class Make something you can
wear Try a circus skills class Have
a white Christmas Eat Mexican food
in Mexico Make a favourite recipe
from when you were a kid Party at
Pikes in Ibiza Find 'The" perfume
or aftershave Watch all Oscar best
pictures Have a food fight Run down
street like Phoebe in Friends Make a
will Start a business Buy an awesome
charity shop outfit Go to Oktoberfest
Go to the chalet from Wham's Last
Christmas video Learn how to Knit
Watch a stage from Tour de France
See Liverpool win The Champions
League Go to Coachella Run to work
Go peroxide blonde Go to Misool See
Orangutans in Borneo Cleanse and
moisturise Cook every recipe from
an old cookbook Graffiti something
See a tennis match at Wimbledon Get
photos printed Float in the Dead
Sea Make up a recipe Have a massive
game of hide and seek Try and learn
a new fact everyday Swim, paddle or
kayak a local river Help someone

solve a problem Donate... anything, blood, time, clothes Give a talk See the pyramids Do a handstand Invent something, even if it's not useful to anyone else Write your name in wet cement Learn how to pick a lock See the Taj Mahal Retire early Attend a talk on something you know nothing about Wave at the Queen Hold a snake Play golf- just once Learn to save someones life Do a Colour Run Drink more water Recreate a childhood photo Learn some basic sign language Rescue an animal Plant a tree Help someone who is sad Say Hello and Thankyou in 10 languages Give up your seat to a stranger Do a Toboggan run (just a little one) Crowd surf Celebrate Songkran in Thailand Go on safari Be a cowboy Ride the Pacific Coast Highway Have a Philly Cheeststeak sarnie in Philladelphia See the day of dead celebrations in Mexico Dance at the Rio carnival Learn Origami Learn to fly Go to a church/mosque/temple Go to The Grand National Learn how to change a tyre Play Roulette in a Casino Meet a World Leader

THESE INVOLVE A CAST OF FAMILY & FRIENDS

Silhouette image: Freepik.com

Go to a music festival Write a poem or song Test drive a car you've always wanted but have no intention of buying Randomly do a cartwheel in public Sing karaoke Repair something Apologise for something you should have a long time ago Do the splits Random act of kindness Ride in a Hot air balloon Try a new sport Try and learn a new language Develop a party trick Perfect a joke Make your own cookbook Sign on as an extra in a film Stay in bed all day See a wonder of the world Get a tattoo Do a Triathlon Sleep under the stars Ride a motorbike Take part in a protest Go to a dance class Run a marathon Skinny dip Draw a moment from your day every day for a year Visit Bora Bora Take time to smell the roses Pay for someone's meal without knowing them Send a message in a bottle Make a loaf of bread Donate blood Shave your head Speak to someone you don't know (every week) Stay in a see-through igloo Write a book Bury some treasure and a note Volunteer Watch the Sunrise & Sunset in one day Find or create

a signature drink Try and learn a musical instrument Try something you hated as a kid Chase a tornado Grow some veg Perfect a recipe Go horse riding on a beach Swim with sharks Visit the place you were born or your first house Fly 1st class Catch a wave Explore a cave Take a gap year Play paintball Send a thank you card to a boss you liked Ride a zip line Stay on a ranch and herd cattle on horseback Walk over hot coals Go on a yacht in Ibiza Go to a drive-in movie Be on a game show Go to bongo's bingo Take silly photos at Madame Tussauds Surprise someone you love Watch the Northern Lights Find someone with your name Swim with Whalesharks Snorkel over a coral reef Get an invite to a Royal event Ride a mechanical rodeo bull Create a family crest Climb a tree Milk a cow Shear a sheep Start a fire without matches Watch baby turtles hatch on a beach Find a friend from junior school Watch an entire box set in one go Go to a black-tie ball Attend something as a VIP Be successful in your

business Jump in pool fully clothed Sell a piece of art Get thrown out of somewhere Dance on a bar Go to an art class Make something you can wear Try a circus skills class Have a white Christmas Eat Mexican food in Mexico Make a favourite recipe from when you were a kid Party at Pikes in Ibiza Find 'The" perfume or aftershave Watch all Oscar best pictures Have a food fight Run down street like Phoebe in Friends Make a will Start a business Buy an awesome charity shop outfit Go to Oktoberfest Go to the chalet from Wham's Last Christmas video Learn how to Knit Watch a stage from Tour de France See Liverpool win The Champions League Go to Coachella Run to work Go peroxide blonde Go to Misool See Orangutans in Borneo Cleanse and moisturise Cook every recipe from an old cookbook Graffiti something See a tennis match at Wimbledon Get photos printed Float in the Dead Sea Make up a recipe Have a massive game of hide and seek Try and learn a new fact everyday Swim, paddle or kayak a local river Help someone

solve a problem Donate... anything, blood, time, clothes Give a talk See the pyramids Do a handstand Invent something, even if it's not useful to anyone else Write your name in wet cement Learn how to pick a lock See the Taj Mahal Retire early Attend a talk on something you know nothing about Wave at the Queen Hold a snake Play golf- just once Learn to save someones life Do a Colour Run Drink more water Recreate a childhood photo Learn some basic sign language Rescue an animal Plant a tree Help someone who is sad Say Hello and Thankyou in 10 languages Give up your seat to a stranger Do a Toboggan run (just a little one) Crowd surf Celebrate Songkran in Thailand Go on safari Be a cowboy Ride the Pacific Coast Highway Have a Philly Cheeststeak sarnie in Philladelphia See the day of dead celebrations in Mexico Dance at the Rio carnival Learn Origami Learn to fly Go to a church/mosque/temple Go to The Grand National Learn how to change a tyre Play Roulette in a Casino Meet a World Leader

THESE WOULD MAKE ME Smile

Go to a music festival Write a poem or song Test drive a car you've always wanted but have no intention of buying Randomly do a cartwheel in public Sing karaoke Repair something Apologise for something you should have a long time ago Do the splits Random act of kindness Ride in a Hot air balloon Try a new sport Try and learn a new language Develop a party trick Perfect a joke Make your own cookbook Sign on as an extra in a film Stay in bed all day See a wonder of the world Get a tattoo Do a Triathlon Sleep under the stars Ride a motorbike Take part in a protest Go to a dance class Run a marathon Skinny dip Draw a moment from your day every day for a year Visit Bora Bora Take time to smell the roses Pay for someone's meal without knowing them Send a message in a bottle Make a loaf of bread Donate blood Shave your head Speak to someone you don't know (every week) Stay in a see-through igloo Write a book Bury some treasure and a note Volunteer Watch the Sunrise & Sunset in one day Find or create

a signature drink Try and learn a musical instrument Try something you hated as a kid Chase a tornado Grow some veg Perfect a recipe Go horse riding on a beach Swim with sharks Visit the place you were born or your first house Fly 1st class Catch a wave Explore a cave Take a gap year Play paintball Send a thank you card to a boss you liked Ride a zip line Stay on a ranch and herd cattle on horseback Walk over hot coals Go on a yacht in Ibiza Go to a drive-in movie Be on a game show Go to bongo's bingo Take silly photos at Madame Tussauds Surprise someone you love Watch the Northern Lights Find someone with your name Swim with Whalesharks Snorkel over a coral reef Get an invite to a Royal event Ride a mechanical rodeo bull Create a family crest Climb a tree Milk a cow Shear a sheep Start a fire without matches Watch baby turtles hatch on a beach Find a friend from junior school Watch an entire box set in one go Go to a black-tie ball Attend something as a VIP Be successful in your

business Jump in pool fully clothed Sell a piece of art Get thrown out of somewhere Dance on a bar Go to an art class Make something you can wear Try a circus skills class Have a white Christmas Eat Mexican food in Mexico Make a favourite recipe from when you were a kid Party at Pikes in Ibiza Find 'The" perfume or aftershave Watch all Oscar best pictures Have a food fight Run down street like Phoebe in Friends Make a will Start a business Buy an awesome charity shop outfit Go to Oktoberfest Go to the chalet from Wham's Last Christmas video Learn how to Knit Watch a stage from Tour de France See Liverpool win The Champions League Go to Coachella Run to work Go peroxide blonde Go to Misool See Orangutans in Borneo Cleanse and moisturise Cook every recipe from an old cookbook Graffiti something See a tennis match at Wimbledon Get photos printed Float in the Dead Sea Make up a recipe Have a massive game of hide and seek Try and learn a new fact everyday Swim, paddle or kayak a local river Help someone

solve a problem Donate... anything, blood, time, clothes Give a talk See the pyramids Do a handstand Invent something, even if it's not useful to anyone else Write your name in wet cement Learn how to pick a lock See the Taj Mahal Retire early Attend a talk on something you know nothing about Wave at the Queen Hold a snake Play golf- just once Learn to save someones life Do a Colour Run Drink more water Recreate a childhood photo Learn some basic sign language Rescue an animal Plant a tree Help someone who is sad Say Hello and Thankyou in 10 languages Give up your seat to a stranger Do a Toboggan run (just a little one) Crowd surf Celebrate Songkran in Thailand Go on safari Be a cowboy Ride the Pacific Coast Highway Have a Philly Cheeststeak sarnie in Philladelphia See the day of dead celebrations in Mexico Dance at the Rio carnival Learn Origami Learn to fly Go to a church/mosque/temple Go to The Grand National Learn how to change a tyre Play Roulette in a Casino Meet a World Leader

Go to a music festival Write a poem or song Test drive a car you've always wanted but have no intention of buying Randomly do a cartwheel in public Sing karaoke Repair something Apologise for something you should have a long time ago Do the splits Random act of kindness Ride in a Hot air balloon Try a new sport Try and learn a new language Develop a party trick Perfect a joke Make your own cookbook Sign on as an extra in a film Stay in bed all day See a wonder of the world Get a tattoo Do a Triathlon Sleep under the stars Ride a motorbike Take part in a protest Go to a dance class Run a marathon Skinny dip Draw a moment from your day every day for a year Visit Bora Bora Take time to smell the roses Pay for someone's meal without knowing them Send a message in a bottle Make a loaf of bread Donate blood Shave your head Speak to someone you don't know (every week) Stay in a see-through igloo Write a book Bury some treasure and a note Volunteer Watch the Sunrise & Sunset in one day Find or create

a signature drink Try and learn a musical instrument Try something you hated as a kid Chase a tornado Grow some veg Perfect a recipe Go horse riding on a beach Swim with sharks Visit the place you were born or your first house Fly 1st class Catch a wave Explore a cave Take a gap year Play paintball Send a thank you card to a boss you liked Ride a zip line Stay on a ranch and herd cattle on horseback Walk over hot coals Go on a yacht in Ibiza Go to a drive-in movie Be on a game show Go to bongo's bingo Take silly photos at Madame Tussauds Surprise someone you love Watch the Northern Lights Find someone with your name Swim with Whalesharks Snorkel over a coral reef Get an invite to a Royal event Ride a mechanical rodeo bull Create a family crest Climb a tree Milk a cow Shear a sheep Start a fire without matches Watch baby turtles hatch on a beach Find a friend from junior school Watch an entire box set in one go Go to a black-tie ball Attend something as a VIP Be successful in your

business Jump in pool fully clothed Sell a piece of art Get thrown out of somewhere Dance on a bar Go to an art class Make something you can wear Try a circus skills class Have a white Christmas Eat Mexican food in Mexico Make a favourite recipe from when you were a kid Party at Pikes in Ibiza Find 'The" perfume or aftershave Watch all Oscar best pictures Have a food fight Run down street like Phoebe in Friends Make a will Start a business Buy an awesome charity shop outfit Go to Oktoberfest Go to the chalet from Wham's Last Christmas video Learn how to Knit Watch a stage from Tour de France See Liverpool win The Champions League Go to Coachella Run to work Go peroxide blonde Go to Misool See Orangutans in Borneo Cleanse and moisturise Cook every recipe from an old cookbook Graffiti something See a tennis match at Wimbledon Get photos printed Float in the Dead Sea Make up a recipe Have a massive game of hide and seek Try and learn a new fact everyday Swim, paddle or kayak a local river Help someone

solve a problem Donate... anything, blood, time, clothes Give a talk See the pyramids Do a handstand Invent something, even if it's not useful to anyone else Write your name in wet cement Learn how to pick a lock See the Taj Mahal Retire early Attend a talk on something you know nothing about Wave at the Queen Hold a snake Play golf- just once Learn to save someones life Do a Colour Run Drink more water Recreate a childhood photo Learn some basic sign language Rescue an animal Plant a tree Help someone who is sad Say Hello and Thankyou in 10 languages Give up your seat to a stranger Do a Toboggan run (just a little one) Crowd surf Celebrate Songkran in Thailand Go on safari Be a cowboy Ride the Pacific Coast Highway Have a Philly Cheeststeak sarnie in Philladelphia See the day of dead celebrations in Mexico Dance at the Rio carnival Learn Origami Learn to fly Go to a church/mosque/temple Go to The Grand National Learn how to change a tyre Play Roulette in a Casino Meet a World Leader

Go to a music festival Write a poem or song Test drive a car you've always wanted but have no intention of buying Randomly do a cartwheel in public Sing karaoke Repair something Apologise for something you should have a long time ago Do the splits Random act of kindness Ride in a Hot air balloon Try a new sport Try and learn a new language Develop a party trick Perfect a joke Make your own cookbook Sign on as an extra in a film Stay in bed all day See a wonder of the world Get a tattoo Do a Triathlon Sleep under the stars Ride a motorbike Take part in a protest Go to a dance class Run a marathon Skinny dip Draw a moment from your day every day for a year Visit Bora bora Take time to smell the roses Pay for someone's meal without knowing them Send a message in a bottle Make a loaf of bread Donate blood Shave your head Speak to someone you don't know (every week) Stay in a see-through igloo Write a book Bury some treasure and a note Volunteer Watch the Sunrise & Sunset in one day Find or create

a signature drink Try and learn a musical instrument Try something you hated as a kid Chase a tornado Grow some veg Perfect a recipe Go horse riding on a beach Swim with sharks Visit the place you were born or your first house Fly 1st class Catch a wave Explore a cave Take a gap year Play paintball Send a thank you card to a boss you liked Ride a zip line Stay on a ranch and herd cattle on horseback Walk over hot coals Go on a yacht in Ibiza Go to a drive-in movie Be on a game show Go to bongo's bingo Take silly photos at Madame Tussauds Surprise someone you love Watch the Northern Lights Find someone with your name Swim with Whalesharks Snorkel over a coral reef Get an invite to a Royal event Ride a mechanical rodeo bull Create a family crest Climb a tree Milk a cow Shear a sheep Start a fire without matches Watch baby turtles hatch on a beach Find a friend from junior school Watch an entire box set in one go Go to a black-tie ball Attend something as a VIP Be successful in your

business Jump in pool fully clothed
Sell a piece of art Get thrown out
of somewhere Dance on a bar Go to
an art class Make something you can
wear Try a circus skills class Have
a white Christmas Eat Mexican food
in Mexico Make a favourite recipe
from when you were a kid Party at
Pikes in Ibiza Find 'The" perfume
or aftershave Watch all Oscar best
pictures Have a food fight Run down
street like Phoebe in Friends Make a
will Start a business Buy an awesome
charity shop outfit Go to Oktoberfest
Go to the chalet from Wham's Last
Christmas video Learn how to Knit
Watch a stage from Tour de France
See Liverpool win The Champions
League Go to Coachella Run to work
Go peroxide blonde Go to Misool See
Orangutans in Borneo Cleanse and
moisturise Cook every recipe from
an old cookbook Graffiti something
See a tennis match at Wimbledon Get
photos printed Float in the Dead
Sea Make up a recipe Have a massive
game of hide and seek Try and learn
a new fact everyday Swim, paddle or
kayak a local river Help someone

solve a problem Donate... anything, blood, time, clothes Give a talk See the pyramids Do a handstand Invent something, even if it's not useful to anyone else Write your name in wet cement Learn how to pick a lock See the Taj Mahal Retire early Attend a talk on something you know nothing about Wave at the Queen Hold a snake Play golf- just once Learn to save someones life Do a Colour Run Drink more water Recreate a childhood photo Learn some basic sign language Rescue an animal Plant a tree Help someone who is sad Say Hello and Thankyou in 10 languages Give up your seat to a stranger Do a Toboggan run (just a little one) Crowd surf Celebrate Songkran in Thailand Go on safari Be a cowboy Ride the Pacific Coast Highway Have a Philly Cheeststeak sarnie in Philladelphia See the day of dead celebrations in Mexico Dance at the Rio carnival Learn Origami Learn to fly Go to a church/mosque/temple Go to The Grand National Learn how to change a tyre Play Roulette in a Casino Meet a World Leader

Go to a music festival Write a poem or song Test drive a car you've always wanted but have no intention of buying Randomly do a cartwheel in public Sing karaoke Repair something Apologise for something you should have a long time ago Do the splits Random act of kindness Ride in a Hot air balloon Try a new sport Try and learn a new language Develop a party trick Perfect a joke Make your own cookbook Sign on as an extra in a film Stay in bed all day See a wonder of the world Get a tattoo Do a Triathlon Sleep under the stars Ride a motorbike Take part in a protest Go to a dance class Run a marathon Skinny dip Draw a moment from your day every day for a year Visit Bora Bora Take time to smell the roses Pay for someone's meal without knowing them Send a message in a bottle Make a loaf of bread Donate blood Shave your head Speak to someone you don't know (every week) Stay in a see-through igloo Write a book Bury some treasure and a note Volunteer Watch the Sunrise & Sunset in one day Find or create

a signature drink Try and learn a musical instrument Try something you hated as a kid Chase a tornado Grow some veg Perfect a recipe Go horse riding on a beach Swim with sharks Visit the place you were born or your first house Fly 1st class Catch a wave Explore a cave Take a gap year Play paintball Send a thank you card to a boss you liked Ride a zip line Stay on a ranch and herd cattle on horseback Walk over hot coals Go on a yacht in Ibiza Go to a drive-in movie Be on a game show Go to bongo's bingo Take silly photos at Madame Tussauds Surprise someone you love Watch the Northern Lights Find someone with your name Swim with Whalesharks Snorkel over a coral reef Get an invite to a Royal event Ride a mechanical rodeo bull Create a family crest Climb a tree Milk a cow Shear a sheep Start a fire without matches Watch baby turtles hatch on a beach Find a friend from junior school Watch an entire box set in one go Go to a black-tie ball Attend something as a VIP Be successful in your

business Jump in pool fully clothed Sell a piece of art Get thrown out of somewhere Dance on a bar Go to an art class Make something you can wear Try a circus skills class Have a white Christmas Eat Mexican food in Mexico Make a favourite recipe from when you were a kid Party at Pikes in Ibiza Find 'The" perfume or aftershave Watch all Oscar best pictures Have a food fight Run down street like Phoebe in Friends Make a will Start a business Buy an awesome charity shop outfit Go to Oktoberfest Go to the chalet from Wham's Last Christmas video Learn how to Knit Watch a stage from Tour de France See Liverpool win The Champions League Go to Coachella Run to work Go peroxide blonde Go to Misool See Orangutans in Borneo Cleanse and moisturise Cook every recipe from an old cookbook Graffiti something See a tennis match at Wimbledon Get photos printed Float in the Dead Sea Make up a recipe Have a massive game of hide and seek Try and learn a new fact everyday Swim, paddle or kayak a local river Help someone

solve a problem Donate... anything, blood, time, clothes Give a talk See the pyramids Do a handstand Invent something, even if it's not useful to anyone else Write your name in wet cement Learn how to pick a lock See the Taj Mahal Retire early Attend a talk on something you know nothing about Wave at the Queen Hold a snake Play golf- just once Learn to save someones life Do a Colour Run Drink more water Recreate a childhood photo Learn some basic sign language Rescue an animal Plant a tree Help someone who is sad Say Hello and Thankyou in 10 languages Give up your seat to a stranger Do a Toboggan run (just a little one) Crowd surf Celebrate Songkran in Thailand Go on safari be a cowboy Ride the Pacific Coast Highway Have a Philly Cheeststeak sarnie in Philladelphia See the day of dead celebrations in Mexico Dance at the Rio carnival Learn Origami Learn to fly Go to a church/mosque/temple Go to The Grand National Learn how to change a tyre Play Roulette in a Casino Meet a World Leader

Go to a music festival Write a poem or song Test drive a car you've always wanted but have no intention of buying Randomly do a cartwheel in public Sing karaoke Repair something Apologise for something you should have a long time ago Do the splits Random act of kindness Ride in a Hot air balloon Try a new sport Try and learn a new language Develop a party trick Perfect a joke Make your own cookbook Sign on as an extra in a film Stay in bed all day See a wonder of the world Get a tattoo Do a Triathlon Sleep under the stars Ride a motorbike Take part in a protest Go to a dance class Run a marathon Skinny dip Draw a moment from your day every day for a year Visit Bora Bora Take time to smell the roses Pay for someone's meal without knowing them Send a message in a bottle Make a loaf of bread Donate blood Shave your head Speak to someone you don't know (every week) Stay in a see-through igloo Write a book Bury some treasure and a note Volunteer Watch the Sunrise & Sunset in one day Find or create

a signature drink Try and learn a musical instrument Try something you hated as a kid Chase a tornado Grow some veg Perfect a recipe Go horse riding on a beach Swim with sharks Visit the place you were born or your first house Fly 1st class Catch a wave Explore a cave Take a gap year Play paintball Send a thank you card to a boss you liked Ride a zip line Stay on a ranch and herd cattle on horseback Walk over hot coals Go on a yacht in Ibiza Go to a drive-in movie Be on a game show Go to bongo's bingo Take silly photos at Madame Tussauds Surprise someone you love Watch the Northern Lights Find someone with your name Swim with Whalesharks Snorkel over a coral reef Get an invite to a Royal event Ride a mechanical rodeo bull Create a family crest Climb a tree Milk a cow Shear a sheep Start a fire without matches Watch baby turtles hatch on a beach Find a friend from junior school Watch an entire box set in one go Go to a black-tie ball Attend something as a VIP Be successful in your

business Jump in pool fully clothed
Sell a piece of art Get thrown out
of somewhere Dance on a bar Go to
an art class Make something you can
wear Try a circus skills class Have
a white Christmas Eat Mexican food
in Mexico Make a favourite recipe
from when you were a kid Party at
Pikes in Ibiza Find 'The" perfume
or aftershave Watch all Oscar best
pictures Have a food fight Run down
street like Phoebe in Friends Make a
will Start a business Buy an awesome
charity shop outfit Go to Oktoberfest
Go to the chalet from Wham's Last
Christmas video Learn how to Knit
Watch a stage from Tour de France
See Liverpool win The Champions
League Go to Coachella Run to work
Go peroxide blonde Go to Misool See
Orangutans in Borneo Cleanse and
moisturise Cook every recipe from
an old cookbook Graffiti something
See a tennis match at Wimbledon Get
photos printed Float in the Dead
Sea Make up a recipe Have a massive
game of hide and seek Try and learn
a new fact everyday Swim, paddle or
kayak a local river Help someone

solve a problem Donate... anything, blood, time, clothes Give a talk See the pyramids Do a handstand Invent something, even if it's not useful to anyone else Write your name in wet cement Learn how to pick a lock See the Taj Mahal Retire early Attend a talk on something you know nothing about Wave at the Queen Hold a snake Play golf- just once Learn to save someones life Do a Colour Run Drink more water Recreate a childhood photo Learn some basic sign language Rescue an animal Plant a tree Help someone who is sad Say Hello and Thankyou in 10 languages Give up your seat to a stranger Do a Toboggan run (just a little one) Crowd surf Celebrate Songkran in Thailand Go on safari be a cowboy Ride the Pacific Coast Highway Have a Philly Cheesesteak sarnie in Philladelphia See the day of dead celebrations in Mexico Dance at the Rio carnival Learn Origami Learn to fly Go to a church/mosque/ temple Go to The Grand National Learn how to change a tyre Play Roulette in a Casino Meet a World Leader

Go to a music festival Write a poem or song Test drive a car you've always wanted but have no intention of buying Randomly do a cartwheel in public Sing karaoke Repair something Apologise for something you should have a long time ago Do the splits Random act of kindness Ride in a Hot air balloon Try a new sport Try and learn a new language Develop a party trick Perfect a joke Make your own cookbook Sign on as an extra in a film Stay in bed all day See a wonder of the world Get a tattoo Do a Triathlon Sleep under the stars Ride a motorbike Take part in a protest Go to a dance class Run a marathon Skinny dip Draw a moment from your day every day for a year Visit Bora Bora Take time to smell the roses Pay for someone's meal without knowing them Send a message in a bottle Make a loaf of bread Donate blood Shave your head Speak to someone you don't know (every week) Stay in a see-through igloo Write a book Bury some treasure and a note Volunteer Watch the Sunrise & Sunset in one day Find or create

a signature drink Try and learn a musical instrument Try something you hated as a kid Chase a tornado Grow some veg Perfect a recipe Go horse riding on a beach Swim with sharks Visit the place you were born or your first house Fly 1st class Catch a wave Explore a cave Take a gap year Play paintball Send a thank you card to a boss you liked Ride a zip line Stay on a ranch and herd cattle on horseback Walk over hot coals Go on a yacht in Ibiza Go to a drive-in movie Be on a game show Go to bongo's bingo Take silly photos at Madame Tussauds Surprise someone you love Watch the Northern Lights Find someone with your name Swim with Whalesharks Snorkel over a coral reef Get an invite to a Royal event Ride a mechanical rodeo bull Create a family crest Climb a tree Milk a cow Shear a sheep Start a fire without matches Watch baby turtles hatch on a beach Find a friend from junior school Watch an entire box set in one go Go to a black-tie ball Attend something as a VIP Be successful in your

business Jump in pool fully clothed Sell a piece of art Get thrown out of somewhere Dance on a bar Go to an art class Make something you can wear Try a circus skills class Have a white Christmas Eat Mexican food in Mexico Make a favourite recipe from when you were a kid Party at Pikes in Ibiza Find 'The" perfume or aftershave Watch all Oscar best pictures Have a food fight Run down street like Phoebe in Friends Make a will Start a business Buy an awesome charity shop outfit Go to Oktoberfest Go to the chalet from Wham's Last Christmas video Learn how to Knit Watch a stage from Tour de France See Liverpool win The Champions League Go to Coachella Run to work Go peroxide blonde Go to Misool See Orangutans in Borneo Cleanse and moisturise Cook every recipe from an old cookbook Graffiti something See a tennis match at Wimbledon Get photos printed Float in the Dead Sea Make up a recipe Have a massive game of hide and seek Try and learn a new fact everyday Swim, paddle or kayak a local river Help someone

solve a problem Donate... anything, blood, time, clothes Give a talk See the pyramids Do a handstand Invent something, even if it's not useful to anyone else Write your name in wet cement Learn how to pick a lock See the Taj Mahal Retire early Attend a talk on something you know nothing about Wave at the Queen Hold a snake Play golf- just once Learn to save someones life Do a Colour Run Drink more water Recreate a childhood photo Learn some basic sign language Rescue an animal Plant a tree Help someone who is sad Say Hello and Thankyou in 10 languages Give up your seat to a stranger Do a Toboggan run (just a little one) Crowd surf Celebrate Songkran in Thailand Go on safari Be a cowboy Ride the Pacific Coast Highway Have a Philly Cheeststeak sarnie in Philladelphia See the day of dead celebrations in Mexico Dance at the Rio carnival Learn Origami Learn to fly Go to a church/mosque/ temple Go to The Grand National Learn how to change a tyre Play Roulette in a Casino Meet a World Leader

THESE CO$T NOTHING

Go to a music festival Write a poem or song Test drive a car you've always wanted but have no intention of buying Randomly do a cartwheel in public Sing karaoke Repair something Apologise for something you should have a long time ago Do the splits Random act of kindness Ride in a Hot air balloon Try a new sport Try and learn a new language Develop a party trick Perfect a joke Make your own cookbook Sign on as an extra in a film Stay in bed all day See a wonder of the world Get a tattoo Do a Triathlon Sleep under the stars Ride a motorbike Take part in a protest Go to a dance class Run a marathon Skinny dip Draw a moment from your day every day for a year Visit Bora Bora Take time to smell the roses Pay for someone's meal without knowing them Send a message in a bottle Make a loaf of bread Donate blood Shave your head Speak to someone you don't know (every week) Stay in a see-through igloo Write a book Bury some treasure and a note Volunteer Watch the Sunrise & Sunset in one day Find or create

a signature drink Try and learn a musical instrument Try something you hated as a kid Chase a tornado Grow some veg Perfect a recipe Go horse riding on a beach Swim with sharks Visit the place you were born or your first house Fly 1st class Catch a wave Explore a cave Take a gap year Play paintball Send a thank you card to a boss you liked Ride a zip line Stay on a ranch and herd cattle on horseback Walk over hot coals Go on a yacht in Ibiza Go to a drive-in movie Be on a game show Go to bongo's bingo Take silly photos at Madame Tussauds Surprise someone you love Watch the Northern Lights Find someone with your name Swim with Whalesharks Snorkel over a coral reef Get an invite to a Royal event Ride a mechanical rodeo bull Create a family crest Climb a tree Milk a cow Shear a sheep Start a fire without matches Watch baby turtles hatch on a beach Find a friend from junior school Watch an entire box set in one go Go to a black-tie ball Attend something as a VIP Be successful in your

business Jump in pool fully clothed
Sell a piece of art Get thrown out
of somewhere Dance on a bar Go to
an art class Make something you can
wear Try a circus skills class Have
a white Christmas Eat Mexican food
in Mexico Make a favourite recipe
from when you were a kid Party at
Pikes in Ibiza Find 'The" perfume
or aftershave Watch all Oscar best
pictures Have a food fight Run down
street like Phoebe in Friends Make a
will Start a business Buy an awesome
charity shop outfit Go to Oktoberfest
Go to the chalet from Wham's Last
Christmas video Learn how to Knit
Watch a stage from Tour de France
See Liverpool win The Champions
League Go to Coachella Run to work
Go peroxide blonde Go to Misool See
Orangutans in Borneo Cleanse and
moisturise Cook every recipe from
an old cookbook Graffiti something
See a tennis match at Wimbledon Get
photos printed Float in the Dead
Sea Make up a recipe Have a massive
game of hide and seek Try and learn
a new fact everyday Swim, paddle or
kayak a local river Help someone

solve a problem Donate... anything, blood, time, clothes Give a talk See the pyramids Do a handstand Invent something, even if it's not useful to anyone else Write your name in wet cement Learn how to pick a lock See the Taj Mahal Retire early Attend a talk on something you know nothing about Wave at the Queen Hold a snake Play golf- just once Learn to save someones life Do a Colour Run Drink more water Recreate a childhood photo Learn some basic sign language Rescue an animal Plant a tree Help someone who is sad Say Hello and Thankyou in 10 languages Give up your seat to a stranger Do a Toboggan run (just a little one) Crowd surf Celebrate Songkran in Thailand Go on safari Be a cowboy Ride the Pacific Coast Highway Have a Philly Cheeststeak sarnie in Philladelphia See the day of dead celebrations in Mexico Dance at the Rio carnival Learn Origami Learn to fly Go to a church/mosque/temple Go to The Grand National Learn how to change a tyre Play Roulette in a Casino Meet a World Leader

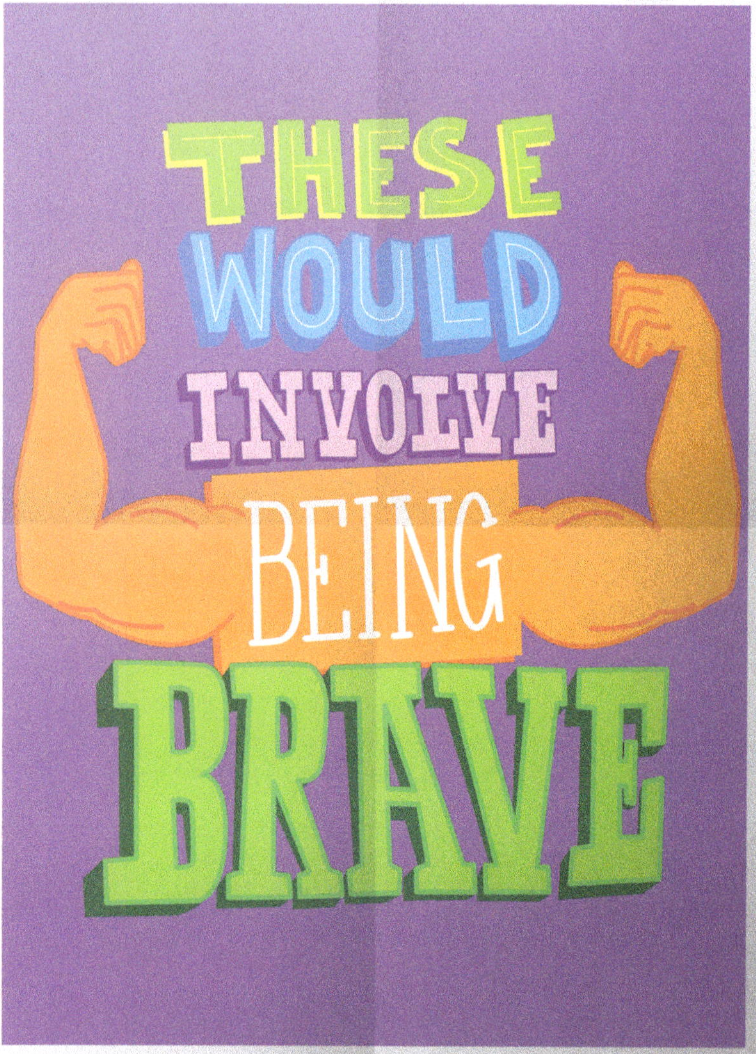
THESE
WOULD
INVOLVE
BEING
BRAVE

Go to a music festival Write a poem or song Test drive a car you've always wanted but have no intention of buying Randomly do a cartwheel in public Sing karaoke Repair something Apologise for something you should have a long time ago Do the splits Random act of kindness Ride in a Hot air balloon Try a new sport Try and learn a new language Develop a party trick Perfect a joke Make your own cookbook Sign on as an extra in a film Stay in bed all day See a wonder of the world Get a tattoo Do a Triathlon Sleep under the stars Ride a motorbike Take part in a protest Go to a dance class Run a marathon Skinny dip Draw a moment from your day every day for a year Visit Bora Bora Take time to smell the roses Pay for someone's meal without knowing them Send a message in a bottle Make a loaf of bread Donate blood Shave your head Speak to someone you don't know (every week) Stay in a see-through igloo Write a book Bury some treasure and a note Volunteer Watch the Sunrise & Sunset in one day Find or create

a signature drink Try and learn a musical instrument Try something you hated as a kid Chase a tornado Grow some veg Perfect a recipe Go horse riding on a beach Swim with sharks Visit the place you were born or your first house Fly 1st class Catch a wave Explore a cave Take a gap year Play paintball Send a thank you card to a boss you liked Ride a zip line Stay on a ranch and herd cattle on horseback Walk over hot coals Go on a yacht in Ibiza Go to a drive-in movie Be on a game show Go to bongo's bingo Take silly photos at Madame Tussauds Surprise someone you love Watch the Northern Lights Find someone with your name Swim with Whalesharks Snorkel over a coral reef Get an invite to a Royal event Ride a mechanical rodeo bull Create a family crest Climb a tree Milk a cow Shear a sheep Start a fire without matches Watch baby turtles hatch on a beach Find a friend from junior school Watch an entire box set in one go Go to a black-tie ball Attend something as a VIP Be successful in your

business Jump in pool fully clothed Sell a piece of art Get thrown out of somewhere Dance on a bar Go to an art class Make something you can wear Try a circus skills class Have a white Christmas Eat Mexican food in Mexico Make a favourite recipe from when you were a kid Party at Pikes in Ibiza Find 'The" perfume or aftershave Watch all Oscar best pictures Have a food fight Run down street like Phoebe in Friends Make a will Start a business Buy an awesome charity shop outfit Go to Oktoberfest Go to the chalet from Wham's Last Christmas video Learn how to Knit Watch a stage from Tour de France See Liverpool win The Champions League Go to Coachella Run to work Go peroxide blonde Go to Misool See Orangutans in Borneo Cleanse and moisturise Cook every recipe from an old cookbook Graffiti something See a tennis match at Wimbledon Get photos printed Float in the Dead Sea Make up a recipe Have a massive game of hide and seek Try and learn a new fact everyday Swim, paddle or kayak a local river Help someone

solve a problem Donate... anything, blood, time, clothes Give a talk See the pyramids Do a handstand Invent something, even if it's not useful to anyone else Write your name in wet cement Learn how to pick a lock See the Taj Mahal Retire early Attend a talk on something you know nothing about Wave at the Queen Hold a snake Play golf- just once Learn to save someones life Do a Colour Run Drink more water Recreate a childhood photo Learn some basic sign language Rescue an animal Plant a tree Help someone who is sad Say Hello and Thankyou in 10 languages Give up your seat to a stranger Do a Toboggan run (just a little one) Crowd surf Celebrate Songkran in Thailand Go on safari Be a cowboy Ride the Pacific Coast Highway Have a Philly Cheeststeak sarnie in Philladelphia See the day of dead celebrations in Mexico Dance at the Rio carnival Learn Origami Learn to fly Go to a church/mosque/ temple Go to The Grand National Learn how to change a tyre Play Roulette in a Casino Meet a World Leader

www.ingramcontent.com/pod-product-compliance
Lightning Source LLC
Chambersburg PA
CBHW040252090526
44586CB00041B/2785